Workb

for

GET OUT OF YOUR HEAD

By JENNIE ALLEN

Stopping the Spiral of Toxic Thoughts

Prepared By

TeamWork Publishers

Workbook for
GET OUT OF YOUR HEAD
By JENNIE ALLEN

Stopping the Spiral of
Toxic Thoughts

Prepared By

TeamWork Publishers

Copyright © June 2020

All rights reserved

Contents

Recommended Books

Prayer Journal: A 3-months guide to Prayer, Praise, and Gratitude featuring encouraging and faith-filled Bible verses

Link: mybook.to/MyPrayerJournal

Gratitude Journal: A Journal filled with Favorite Bible Verses

Link: mybook.to/GratitudeJournal

Introduction

Jennie's work is a gift for Christians struggling to live a life free from worry, doubt, anxiety, and fear, but don't know how to go about it. Jennie is saying that the limitations are all in your head and you should get out of there and become who you were destined to be in God. According to Jennie, the toxic thoughts in our head and the belief we have of them keep us in bondage, and until we break from them, we will always be held captive and limited.

In her work, Jennie explains how our beliefs affect us and how we can break free from them and make progress in life. Breaking free from our toxic thoughts involves identifying these thoughts and drawing the battle line against them.

However, waging war against this nature of enemy requires a little of your effort and more of God's power as lifting the load with God guarantees victory. We must choose to be still with God, surrendering all our fears and delighting in Him. We must choose to be grateful irrespective of our challenges and seek the good of others as we can't find fulfillment when focusing on ourselves alone.

Jennie, in her book, also talks about how we can think like Jesus. This is very important because we have always focused on our troubles.

This workbook is designed to help you assimilate the ideas of Jennie Allen in her book, "Get out of your head." Being a workbook, it contains exercises aim at taking captive of all toxic thoughts in your head and molding a completely new heart and person out of you. Some tasks may require you to leave your comfort zone and reach out to people. Make sure you do them.

This workbook is also designed in such a way that as you take on the exercises, and in line with the author's principles, you will discover where you got things wrong and how you can help yourself. Make up your mind to yield yourself wholly to this material, and your life would never remain the same again.

You will only begin to see positive changes in your life when you take bold steps to go in the direction of this workbook.

Part 1: All The Thoughts

1 Thinking About Thinking

Have you ever sit to reflect on your thoughts? Have you ever asked yourself why you think the way you do? Negative thoughts, when left unchecked, can cripple everything about us in the long run. As pointed out by Jennie, it all begins with one area of your life and spiral out to other areas.

Jennie, in the first line of her work, says, "Take every thought captive." What does that mean to you? It means you should be ready to deal with what comes into your head. If you don't, the negative thoughts may start with ruining a day going into a week, a week translating to a month, and finally, you are ruined.

You can escape the downward spiral by shifting your thinking and becoming happy with your life irrespective of what you feel that you are not good at or the criticisms thrown at you. You can choose never to be a victim of your thought, but a warrior equipped to fight the battle of the mind—the greatest battle of our generation.

Through research, Jennie established that our lives are defined by the emotions we pick up, leading to thoughts, which dictate our decisions that determine how we behave, and by extension, the relationship we develop or keep. Ultimately, our relationships would create emotions, leading us to thoughts, and the cycle continues.

For Jennie, all we've been trying to do is fixing symptoms instead of the root problem, which is about how we think, which creates the emotions.

This means that if we can do something about the way we think, we can create the life that we want to live, or become transformed as we take charge of our thoughts. Such transformation can be in business, career, health, or otherwise.

Exercise

Do you find yourself moving in and out of a bad thought, relationship, or habit?

_____

_____

If yes, what are they?

_____

_____

_____

_____

_____

_____

Have you been trying to get unstuck or break from these things?

_____

_____

If yes, what have you done or currently doing?

_____

_____

_____

_____

What success did you record or recording?

_____

_____

_____

_____

Ever found yourself brooding over thoughts and then someone try talking you out of it, yet you find yourself going over the thought again? Can you describe the situation?

_____

_____

_____

_____

_____

What do you think was responsible for your inability to break from your bad thoughts, relationship, or habit irrespective of your efforts to do so?

_____

_____

_____

_____

Write down 10 things in your mind right now.

_____

_____

_____

_____

_____

_____

_____

_____

_____

_____

_____

From your list, write down the thoughts you can judge are healthy: good before God and man.

_____

_____

_____

_____

_____

_____

_____

_____

From your list, write down the thoughts you can judge are unhealthy: bad before God and man.

_____

_____

_____

_____

_____

_____

_____

_____

_____

_____

From the list of your healthy thoughts, which thought is <u>most important</u> to you right now?

_____

_____

_____

_____

_____

List your action points to fix this thought.

_____

_____

_____

_____

_____

_____

_____

Tip: Focus your energy to do everything about this thought before thinking about something else. Think about this one thing until you've achieved what you need from it. If a thought is for the future, mark or record it on your calendar and take your mind away from it. Refuse to bug your head with thoughts, especially those unhealthy ones.

In your leisure, or idle time, list 5 healthy thoughts you can always reflect on instead of allowing your mind to roam?

_____

_____

_____

_____

_____

_____

_____

_____

Tip: The things on this list should replace those of the unhealthy thought list.

2 What We Believe

Our life is shaped by the things we believe about ourselves. Such things may be true or lies, and until we change our belief system, we can never change our life.

Jennie Allen, in her book, talks about the lies she believed about herself at some point in life. She built her life around these lies, and they affected her immensely. However, the time came that she realized these lies and, then she decided to change her belief and, in the process, changed her life.

Jennie categorized the lies we all tell ourselves.

These include;

I am helpless.
I am worthless.
I am unlovable.

However, according to Jennie, the lies we believe about ourselves only reveals our level of relationship with God. When we don't believe what God says about us, we end up believing the things we say about ourselves.

Believing that we are helpless invariably means that we can't draw from God's strength to create changes.

Believing that we are worthless means that God's creation isn't worthy, and we were not created in His image.

And believing we are unlovable means that God isn't telling us the truth and has been lying about telling us that He loves us.

These are the lies from the pit of hell that we believe.

The good news is that we can change our wrong beliefs by accepting and meditating on what God says about us, which is the truth.

Exercise

Go in front of a mirror and look at yourself once again. Write five things that you believe about yourself.

_____

_____

_____

_____

_____

_____

_____

_____

From the list above, what items is in line with
God's Word about us and what is not?

_____

_____

_____

_____

_____

_____

Which of the three lies as pointed out by the author
have you fallen a victim?

_____

_____

_____

_____

_____

How did you get yourself off the lie(s)?

_____

_____

_____

_____

_____

_____

Do you still believe this lie(s)?

_____

_____

_____

_____

What truth in God's Word counters these fundamental lies? Write down the Bible verses that support these truths.

_____

_____

_____

_____

From these Bible verses, write down six positive affirmations (two for each lie). Say and meditate on them daily.

_____

_____

_____

_____

_____

_____

_____

3 Spiraling Out

Jennie had suffered anxiety and worry about the existence of God due to situations in her life at a point in time.

She worried a lot and doubted God's love for her, including His existence. She lost sleep and was falling into depression.

Soon, she was under attack, and that got her crippled, and for once, she began to believe that the idea of God was made to deceive. She thought once she's dead, her life would end right there.

But she was famous for her pro-Christian stand through her books and as a speaker. Yet, she was caught in the web of doubt and negative spiral thoughts.

One day, she re-discovered herself. She realized where she got it all wrong with life. She embraced her doubts instead of fighting to overcome them with the instrument of God's Word.

When we focus on our doubts and worries without seeking and believing the truth, we invite anxiety and depression into our life, and these two are up to no good.

Exercise

Have you ever fallen for anxiety and depression?

_____

_____

_____

_____

_____

_____

If yes, can you give account of how your thoughts led you to anxiety and depression?

_____

_____

_____

_____

_____

_____

_____

_____

_____

Looking back today, where did you get it all wrong?

_____

_____

_____

_____

_____

_____

Have you ever doubted God's existence or His love
for you?

_____

_____

_____

If yes, what experience led to your doubt and
unbelief about Him?

_____

_____

_____

_____

_____

_____

How do you express your trust in God in your words, thoughts and actions?

_____

_____

_____

_____

_____

_____

_____

_____

What do you do when thoughts and emotions seem to take you on a ride?

_____

_____

_____

_____

_____

_____

How do you know what thought or doubt to entertain in your mind?

_____

_____

_____

_____

_____

What hope lies in the Word of God for you considering your most common doubts? Search the scriptures.

_____

_____

_____

_____

_____

_____

_____

_____

_____

4 Breaking Free

A point came in Jennie's life when she was no longer at ease with her faith in God even though she tried as much as she could to keep believing. Finally, she confessed to her friends about what had happened to her faith in God—she couldn't believe God again. Her friends couldn't believe her confession because they had known her as someone who was very strong in her faith.

Jennie's final fall into doubts and uncertainty happened when she attended a conference in Uganda, but something surprising to her happened. In the meeting, Psalm 139 was recited during a devotional session. This scripture happened to be one she had memorized and used to meditate on it in the past.

The author was surprised to realize that of all the verses in the Bible, Psalm 139 was recited while she was there and during a time her faith in God seems to fail. Suddenly, she began to recollect herself and realized that it was the devil trying to take her away from God using the evil power of doubts and uncertainty. Immediately, she made up her mind to fight Satan off her life and return to God.

Going through the dark times, Jennie wasn't alone. She had friends that strengthen her faith through fasting and praying. This explains the need for community.

The author also posits that anxiety or depression can be treated medically. There shouldn't be any shame in doing so, but where medication fails may mean that the devil is waging war against us, and such war can only be won by looking to God and His Word.

Exercise

Do you have friends that encourage you to keep the faith when life seems not to go as planned?

_____

_____

_____

_____

_____

How do you fight back the devil when he comes to you with doubt and uncertainty?

_____

_____

_____

_____

_____

What favorite scripture do you use to comfort yourself when doubts seem to overwhelm you?

_____

_____

_____

_____

_____

_____

_____

_____

_____

5 Where Thoughts Are Captured

We are faced with the challenge of thoughts running through our minds. However, we can't allow these thoughts go through us uncontrollably. We must filter and drop all negative thoughts else they cripple us.

We can refine every thought that enters our minds. Failure to take charge of our thoughts would see us living a less focused and organized life.

The things that go through our minds create our emotions. The emotions mold our behavior while our behaviors create our relationships. This means that to affect the whole spiral, we need to deal with our thoughts. We can choose to yield to the negative thoughts or reject them.

We are not helpless because Jesus Christ has given us the power of choice. We are fully in charge of everything that happens within us. You don't allow your thoughts to take charge of you, but you take charge of them. Always remember that what we think, we become. Hence, when negative thoughts arise in your mind, drop them immediately. If we can correct or redirect our children, we can also do the same with our thoughts.

God's Word is the best antidote to negative thoughts, and anything that doesn't align with what the Word says about us shouldn't be taken to heart. Having our minds saturated with the truths of God's Word is one way to suppress the growth of negative thoughts, doubt, or anxiety. Depending on how you respond to God's Word, your thought battle may take a shorter time, and other times longer.

Exercise

What primary thought do you have of God toward you?

_____

_____

_____

_____

_____

_____

What can you say about your relationship with God based on your thought?

_____

_____

_____

_____

_____

_____

What thought about God do you need to hold firmly or drop?

_____

_____

_____

_____

_____

What behavior do you need to change by changing your thought?

_____

_____

_____

_____

_____

What negative thoughts do you choose to drop today so that you can focus more on God?

_____

_____

_____

_____

_____

_____

What are your favorite Bible verses to remind yourself when negative thoughts arise in your mind?

_____

_____

_____

_____

_____

_____

_____

_____

6 Make the Shift

The human mind seems to harbor more negative thoughts than good ones. It's also been established that what we become in life can't be different from our thoughts. Our thoughts create our emotions, which forms our belief system. The belief we have of life and ourselves dictate who we are or what we become in life. Life is this simple!

However, it is not to pretend that all is well, but knowing how to overcome your negative thoughts. You must learn to analyze and take action against every negative thought.

First, draw up a mental story map of how you feel. How do you feel? What makes you feel the way you do? How can you respond to the tiny things that contribute to the major? Write everything down.

Next, talk to God about each item, not just with your words but using scriptures that address your concerns. Biblical prayers release the power of God.

Again, find patterns in your thought and also take them to the feet of Jesus. Whatever may be your want or need, let Jesus know about it.

Instead of worrying and becoming depressed, map your worries and submit them at the feet of Jesus. However, going to Jesus shouldn't only be when you have problems but knowing Him more and developing a cordial relationship with Him so that you can think the way He does. No self-help can beat focusing on Jesus. As you continue to move closer to Him, you become renewed to a brand new person—not subject to negative thoughts but thinking like Jesus.

Exercise

What's the one major thought that's occupying your mind right now?

_____

_____

_____

_____

List the things that are contributing to this thought?

_____

_____

_____

_____

_____

_____

What scripture or God's Word can settle each item on the list?

_____

_____

_____

_____

_____

_____

For each item and scripture, write a prayer on a sticky note and paste them in your closet. Meditate on them every day to keep your mind at peace and focused on God. Expect answers to your prayers.

List the things you can do to focus more on Jesus?

_____

_____

_____

_____

_____

_____

_____

_____

Part 2: Taking Down the Enemies of our Minds

7 Drawing Battle Lines

One of the most important things about winning the war in our minds is knowing when to draw the battle line. Your inability to draw the battle line about harmful thoughts that may be going through your mind can lead to unpleasant consequences.

For Jennie, you are what you think. Your thought can steer you off course and, at the same time, can change your situation for the best. It has nothing to do with the nature of your situation: good or bad, but how you respond to the situation in your mind.

You must be very careful with handling your thoughts because once the devil succeeds to set you up for confusion, it becomes a never-ending stream of negative thoughts with the sole aim of pulling you down. You must become smarter than the devil by having a mental clarity of your thoughts.

The author, in her book, believes that either Satan, our wounds, or sin can set the stage in our minds for a confusion. Through lies that Satan may plant in our brains, we can become confused. To defeat the devil, we must take our thoughts captive.

To take our thoughts captive means remembering and focusing on the truth of God's Word about our lives. However, to remember God's Word means that you must first study and meditate on the Word.

Also, our wounds can lead us to confusion and blur our sense of reasoning. Focusing on your wounds can make you form a belief around it, which may largely be lies. You don't also have to allow the wounds of others to make you believe the circumstances to be true.

Jennie is of the position that our sins can create confusion in our minds. Sin, in simple terms is focusing on the desires of the flesh when we ought to be concentrating on the desires of the Spirit which contains the truth. The astonishing reality is that our flesh lies to us to satisfy her desires while our spirit reveals the truth to us, which brings what we truly desire. While our flesh counts for nothing, our spirit with the guidance of the Holy Spirit of God gives us true peace.

Irrespective of the devices of the devil to get us confused and trapped, we can always come out victorious through Jesus' death and resurrection. The death of Jesus on the Cross brought us victory over Satan and making us fit to take charge of our minds.

Every time you battle with bad thought should remind you about the work you need to do to take in more of God's Word. Without Jesus through His

Word in us, we are bound to be overwhelmed by our thoughts and defected by Satan.

Exercise

What are some of those thoughts that come to you often that you truly know are not of God?

_____

_____

_____

_____

_____

What truths of God's Word can you use to counter each of these thoughts?

_____

_____

_____

_____

_____

_____

_____

For every bad thought listed in (1) above, what two scriptures can you use to counter them?

_____

_____

_____

_____

_____

_____

_____

Do you truly believe that Jesus already won the battle against the devil for you?

Yes [   ] No [   ]

If yes, and considering your bad thoughts in (1) above, how are you going to change your mind through your confessions and actions?

Confessions:

_____

_____

_____

_____

_____

_____

_____

_____

Actions/New behaviors:

_____

_____

_____

_____

_____

_____

_____

What outstanding battle or thought are you facing right now?

_____

_____

_____

_____

_____

What is the truth in God's Word about this thought? Write the scripture(s).

_____

_____

_____

_____

_____

_____

With the above scripture(s) in mind, clearly describe your next line of action to silence all voices of confusion from the devil?

_____

_____

_____

_____

_____

_____

_____

8 Holding Space for Silence

One way you can avoid distractive thoughts is to take care of your mental health. Sound mental health breathes organized thoughts that give birth to an organized life.

Naturally, our minds would keep wandering, except we move closer to God. Drawing closer to God helps us to select and dwell our minds only on the right thoughts. It helps create calmness in our hearts, which culminate in a better focus, less depression and anxiety and positive impacts on our brain.

It shouldn't be hard for you to spend time and take a dose of God's Word every day. Don't leave such an opportunity to organize your life to chance. Do it consciously, and when it's time, shut yourself from all forms of distractions. While there alone, you may choose to pray, meditate on the Word, praise, or worship God.

In life, the devil is constantly throwing thoughts into our minds, and dwelling on those thoughts can lead you to unproductive living or destruction. You can't really achieve anything in life if you can't take charge of your mind. Every time you are faced with distraction in your mind, look up to God— through singing, praying, or meditating on God's Word. You can do any of these quietly in your mind.

Nothing can replace the understanding that God is for you, and if God is for you, what, or who can be against you? Life isn't about brooding over our thoughts but dwelling in God's love, standing still in Him, and taking charge of our thoughts and actions.

Exercise

What biggest distraction usually stops you from having a quiet time with God?

_____

_____

_____

_____

_____

How can you deal with this distraction?

_____

_____

_____

_____

_____

_____

_____

Do you usually find it difficult to yield to God's way of doing things?

_____

_____

_____

_____

_____

_____

If yes, do you think this is a sign that the devil is taking charge of your thoughts and you are yielding to him even though such may not be obvious to you?

_____

_____

_____

_____

Do you have any fear that yielding to thoughts from the Word of God or doing things God's way may be a risk?

_____

_____

_____

Tip: If you are not grounded on the Word of God, it may appear that taking God's instruction is a risk and He may not be there for you when you call on Him.

What immediate steps can you take to draw close to God?

_____

_____

_____

_____

_____

_____

Considering the above, make a weekly plan of having a quiet time with God beginning next week.

Day	Activity	Duration	Venue
Mon			
Tues			
Wed			
Thu			
Fri			
Sat			
Sun			

Your activity could be Bible study, prayer, meditation, singing in hymns, praise and worship.

Venue could be your house, garden, a special quiet place, church, etc.

9 Lifeliness: I Choose To Be Known

Getting out of your head is getting out of your bad and discouraging negative thoughts from building up in your mind. Most times, we become depressed as a result of isolating ourselves due to a negative thought that people don't love us and may not want us around them. Keeping away from others can cause loneliness, which eventually can push us into depression.

God designed us to be seen and known by others. He made us for a relationship with others and not to work alone. He made us to eat and dine with others; to laugh and share our pains with others.

When we form a community with others and open up to them, we take the load off our heart and even if we had some secrets we may have loved to keep within us and even when they trouble us from the inside, the moment we say them out, we become free. You shouldn't be worried about who gets to hear your little secrets, pushing them out of you is better than allowing them to be there for Satan to use and torment you.

There is a greater need to be in a community with others, as stressed by Jennie in this chapter. God in itself exists in community of the Father, Son, and the Holy Spirit, and He has created us to also function in community with others. There are always people who are ready to relate with you irrespective of who you are. Don't allow Satan to deceive you that you can't be loved. Don't isolate yourself. You were made to function with others. The real essence of life is functioning in a community with others. There are people out there that you can impact for good, while they also do the same to you. You can only find help and love when in a community and not when you are isolating yourself. Isolating yourself would give the devil the opportunity to throw negative thoughts into your mind, especially when you have a problem.

When you feel stressed, you need to be with people and not alone else you build up the stress. However, while there is a greater need to bond with others, it's also important to carefully choose who to bond with.

Certain factors must be considered:
1. Are the people strong in their faith?
2. Are they strong in their relationships?
3. Are they strong interpersonally?

Once you can find people with these three qualities, you can form a community with them.

What more? Learn to ask from members of your community—ask for help, ask for anything. And when they also ask from you, don't say no; fight to help them meet their needs.

One thing important when in a community is to be yourself—be original; be free. Don't try to hide anything; else those things would begin to fight you. Don't be afraid of anybody leaving you if they realize who you are for real. The people that genuinely love you would stick around. Those are your real friends. Fortunately, there are always such people.

How do you want others to act toward you? Act toward them the same way. The essence of being in a community is so you can share with them. Don't keep your pains and shame with you, share with your friends—say the last 2%. When you don't share your pains and shame with others, the devil uses them to torment you.

Exercise

How is your community right now? Do you feel it's great or it does need some improvement?

_____

_____

_____

_____

_____

List the people you believe are your real friends.

Rubrics:
    (a)   Are the people strong in their faith?
    (b)   Are they strong in their relationships?
    (c)   Are they strong interpersonally?

_____

_____

_____

_____

_____

Who do you think you should build a community with that is not in the list above?

_____

_____

_____

_____

How do you relate with the people in your community (e.g., social media, physical meeting, phone calls, etc.)?

_____

_____

_____

Which channel of meeting with your friends work well for you and help you to open up?

_____

_____

_____

Is there something you've kept in your heart and you are worried telling people about them may not be the best?

_____

_____

_____

_____

Tip: If yes, and if this little secret gives you concern, it's time to let go of it.

How do you feel when with your friends?

_____

_____

_____

_____

Do you open up when with them?

_____

_____

Do you feel they can betray you?

_____

_____

_____

Who among your friends do you think you need to keep away from?

_____

_____

_____

_____

10 Unafraid: I Choose to Surrender My Fears to God

The fear of failure can drive us into a spiral of thought. Even when we know our strength isn't enough to face the situation, we won't give it up to God but keep being anxious and losing our mind.

When we keep dwelling on 'what if this or that happens,' we deprive God of the ability to take charge of the situation because God can only step in and help us when we stop worrying or thinking about our problems.

We tend to believe the lie from the pit of hell that God doesn't care about us, so we should keep worrying. But worry is only a tool that Satan uses to keep us perpetually distracted so we can't focus on our goals in life. God is always in control, and we need to surrender our fears and anxiety to Him.

Paul admonishes us to be anxious for nothing, but with prayer and thanksgiving, we should make our petition known to God. He says we should give our thought to whatever that is true and noble and pure while giving up our anxieties to God. Instead of thinking about your lack, think of God being your shepherd; instead of thinking about accident, think about abiding under the shadow of the almighty. Surrender your fears to God. Trade your worries for His ability, mercy, and love and be at rest.

Everything that is not consistent or true about God is lies from Satan, and the moment you believe those lies, he begins to reign over your life. You must learn to confront Satan and keep every bad thought he wants you to believe under your feet using the Word of God.

Our anxieties are born of fear. There is nothing wrong with being afraid, but we must cast our concerns to God and believe that He is with us, supporting our position and working out a solution. Don't keep saying, "What do I do?" when there's nothing you can do. Instead, choose to believe God for a way out.

God has a track record of rescuing His children when they call on Him while in distress. Remind yourself of the things He's done in the past and also declare His promises for you as contained in His Word instead of declaring your fears. You can also communicate your fears with your friends and family and seek their prayers. Finally, live in the consciousness that God is with you, and nothing can overwhelm you.

Exercise

What's your biggest fear right now?

_____

_____

_____

_____

What Bible passages dispel this fear?

_____

_____

_____

_____

Can you remember a time in your life that you were so worried but God eventually showed up?

_____

_____

_____

_____

If yes, describe the situation and how God intervened.

_____

_____

_____

_____

What promises of God do you hold firmly about your life?

_____

_____

_____

_____

How can you relate the scripture about the lilies of
the field in Matthew 6:28 to your life?

_____

_____

_____

_____

What can you make of Matthew 6:25-34 when
considering your worries?

_____

_____

_____

_____

Write 10 things that God has done for you in the
past?

_____

_____

_____

_____

_____

_____

_____

Considering the things that God has done for you in the past, do you still have doubt about His ability to intervene in your present situation?

_____

_____

_____

_____

Take a walk into the natural environment devoid of the 'artificials' and surrounded by plants or trees. Make yourself a little comfortable. Make sure you are safe.

Look around and imagine the handwork of God. Imagine the birds, the trees, the blue sky; imagine yourself in the midst of nature. Walk, look around, and imagine how big God is to have created everything around you.

Right there, surrender all and re-dedicate your life to God. Having seen His works and greatness, give up your worries and any time there's a cause to worry, remember how great is our God—far greater than your challenges. Isn't that enough to meditate on Him when you feel challenged?

11 A Beautiful Interruption: I Choose to Delight in God

To be optimistic or cynical is a choice. Optimism is showing up for the future, being joyful, and believing that all things will work out for you, while cynicism is holding a skewed belief that people aren't trustworthy and that things won't work out for your good.

Choosing to be optimistic would keep you away from bad thoughts. Optimism isn't a type of vulnerability but to stay without having toxic thoughts going through your mind. It's a way of trusting and causing nature to favor you. There's no point using cynicism as a protective garment when it's going to stop you from experiencing joy, hope, or trust.

You don't need to trust people but to just love them and trusting only God. And God being trustworthy surely means that your expectations won't be put to shame and all things would work out for your good.

In life, you will be hurt. Everyone feels hurt at one point in their life. No one is exempted. Even the rich also cry. That's just what life is all about. Feeling hurt doesn't mean God shouldn't be trusted. It doesn't mean God can't take care of you or He's not taking care of us, or He doesn't want the best for us. God is God at all times. He is the same yesterday, today and forever. He is good all the time. Hurt shouldn't deprive you of happiness but should only remind you that sometimes, life can tilt to either side: good or bad, joy or sadness. The journey of life hangs between these extremes. You create a balance.

Whatever happens, appreciate the gift of life. Appreciate God's creation. Look around you and see the mighty works of God. Declare His greatness. Declare His love. Speak good about His works. Believe in Him.

You've received Christ into your spirit which is the hope of glory. He is your savior. He is your future. Give no room to cynicism; give no room to fear and anxiety.

Exercise

Looking at your life today, what can possibly make you become cynical?

_____

_____

_____

_____

_____

_____

How can you deal with these things in the light of God's Word?

_____

_____

_____

_____

What usually strikes your mind when you reflect on God's creation and His mighty works?

_____

_____

_____

_____

Do you believe God to be trustworthy based on your personal experience about life?

Yes [ ] No [ ]

If yes, what significant thing happened in your life that boosts your trust in God?

_____

_____

_____

_____

Have you been tempted by the devil to be cynical?

Yes [ ] No [ ]

If yes, describe the experience.

_____

_____

_____

_____

Based on your knowledge of God now, what can you say about your experiences in the past about being cynical?

_____

_____

_____

_____

What does Christ sacrifice mean to you?

_____

_____

_____

_____

_____

_____

12 Less Important: I Choose to Serve God and Others

Having joy in the heart and living freely depends not only on the things that you can do for yourself but also for others. In putting others ahead of us, we become humbled. Humility demands that we give grace to others more than ourselves.

Even though we were born into a culture that focuses on self-glorification, we shouldn't allow it to influence us to choose to follow the ways of Jesus. Jesus served God and others while He walked the earth, and we should choose to do the same. Living a quality life isn't just about amassing wealth and trying to make ourselves happy, but serving can help us to experience real joy. Of course, there are wealthy people that have struggled to find joy but ended up with sadness and depression. Serving God and others may have been what they missed.

Experiencing a better life isn't about trying to rack up self-esteem. We shouldn't believe that this is the way to go because our culture promotes it. It's just a lie. We can't go far with such thought. The real joy in life is found in serving God and others and not focusing on ourselves. Serving God and others is a surefire way of changing our lives for good.

Apostle Paul set a good example in this regard. He denied himself and instead chose to serve God and others, and he was great. You can only achieve then achieved greatness through service—lifting the name of God and others above self. Don't spend so much time trying to measure up with others. This is striving after the wind; instead, let God be the center of your self-worth. Focusing on God and others can help you to build real relationships, but when you choose to focus on yourself, we may end up hurting others and not still able to find joy and happiness.

We must learn to give ourselves to humility and allow our spirit to come to the reality that we are not awesome, and we can't make ourselves awesome, but focusing on God's awesomeness can be our crowning beauty.

Humility would also help us to see people just as God sees them; it will help us to build empathy, and in the process, we will discover ourselves.

Humility is one virtue that we all need to live an organized and satisfying life. Our culture and the world at large don't understand the benefit of sincere humility, and hence, can't reap the benefits thereof, but we Christians do know, especially as our Master, while here on earth was a humble man, and had thought us the essence of humility.

Continue looking up to Jesus and helping others to achieve their purpose in life. That's where true joy lies.

Exercise

How has pride been showing up in you based on
how you've read about and understand it in
Jennie's book?

_____

_____

_____

_____

_____

_____

How have you been able to show humility in your
words and deeds?

    (a)   In your workplace

_____

_____

_____

_____

_____

    (b)   At home

_____

_____

_____

_____

_____

_____

(c)   In your community

_____

_____

_____

_____

_____

(d)   When walking on the streets

_____

_____

_____

_____

(e)   In the church

_____

_____

_____

_____

_____

What new ways can you show humility?

   (a)   In your workplace

_____

_____

_____

_____

_____

   (b)   At home

_____

_____

_____

_____

_____

   (c)   In your community

_____

_____

_____

_____

_____

_____

(d)   When walking on the streets

_____

_____

_____

_____

_____

(e)   In the church

_____

_____

_____

_____

_____

What part of you easily leads you to show pride?
e.g., dressing, words, action, walking, looking, etc.

_____

_____

_____

_____

_____

How do you hope to deal with this weakness?

_____

_____

_____

_____

_____

Have you ever enjoyed humility from others?
Describe a situation that stood out.

_____

_____

_____

_____

_____

Mention 5 ways you can use your gifts/possessions
and talents to serve God?

_____

_____

_____

_____

_____

_____

Make a move. List places or people you can go to visit (e.g. orphanage home) to show or express some humility by way of service to them.

_____

_____

_____

_____

_____

_____

_____

_____

Note: In serving people, you serve God.

13 Not Overcome: I Choose To Be Grateful

Life is full of circumstances that push us to complain, and we all have once found ourselves in a position that we feel like complaining. When you feel that you are not living up to your potential, there's bound to be that urge to complain. However, God knew we would be facing this situation, and through Paul, He warned us to be full of thanksgiving to Him, irrespective of any situation we may find ourselves.

Being grateful even for the little we may have, and giving thanks to God gives us peace and hope that the present situation is bound to change. Your ability to replace your complains with gratitude can also help rewire your brain to think and live healthier.

Jennie identified seven different ways that gratitude rewires our brain.
1. It creates for more relationships.
2. It improves our physical wellbeing.
3. It improves our psychological wellbeing.
4. It improves our sleep.
5. It helps us to see the world from others' perspectives.
6. It helps us to reduce aggression.
7. It improves our mental strength and self-esteem.

The above-mentioned isn't just the idea of the author, but researchers have confirmed them to be true. They are also of the position that the more we can practice gratitude, the more we are likely to be grateful for other things. Indeed, gratitude is good. It's a perfect tool from God to us to help us live in peace with our lives and situations.

Many have already been in the habit of thanksgiving, and that's why you can see people in a worst situation than yours, yet thankful and still believing in life irrespective. You should be able to talk to them how they do even when they are in deeper trouble. Apart from the people in your world, Jennie strongly recommends you study the life of Apostle Paul, who faced so many horrible circumstances but grateful.

On this note, Jennie is advising that you shouldn't allow your circumstances dictate the direction of your life else you will always find yourself complaining about your situation and losing peace of mind and never coming to the realization that you ought to be thankful.

Generally, without our experiences, we will never see or have regard for the blessing of God upon our lives. We must be thankful irrespective of what we go through in life.

The fight of life isn't ours but one with Jesus. We can only win in our endeavors with Jesus on our side—not our strength but His' working through us. Don't develop a victim mindset when going through tough times. You are not a victim in Jesus. A victim mentality can only lead you to develop toxic thoughts and becoming restless. Trust that God has plans for you, and He is aware of what you may be going through at any point in time. He knows beforehand that you will face the difficulties that you do. This makes your worries and fears totally unnecessary.

Instead of complaining, see how you can glorify God in your challenges and be thankful for your past victories in Him. Being grateful for what He's given or done for you in the past makes way for your present difficulties. God's plan toward us is always good irrespective of what our present circumstances may be saying.

Exercise

Ever found yourself in a position that pushes you to complain and/or doubt your believe in God?
Yes [ ]   No [ ]

If yes, what was it like? Looking back today, what can you learn from that situation?

_____

_____

_____

_____

_____

Which benefit of being grateful listed by the author do you truly believe is true and have been working for you?

_____

_____

_____

_____

_____

How do you express gratitude to God on a daily basis?

_____

_____

_____

_____

_____

Do you keep a record of God's goodness to you?

Yes [ ] No [ ]

If yes, do you find peace and joy when you see or feel those things that God has done for you?

Yes [ ] No [ ]

Do you believe that being grateful can bring you inner peace and make you receive more from God?

Yes [ ] No [ ]

If yes, how do you hope to improve your attitude of thanksgiving to God?

_____

_____

_____

_____

_____

_____

Can you remember any time you've been grateful to God in the face of your difficulties?

Yes [ ] No [ ]

Mention three ways you can be thankful to God irrespective of your troubles?

_____

_____

_____

_____

_____

What five key things in your life make you eternally thankful to God?

_____

_____

_____

_____

_____

_____

_____

_____

_____

_____

14 Run Your Race: I Choose to Seek the Good of Others

God designed life in such a way that we cannot find fulfillment when we live outside of Him. This is the reason why we seem to become tired of life and care less about anything. When we live for ourselves, suddenly, life seems not to make sense again because of situations that we may have to face.

We were designed to live for God and living for God is living for others. We can achieve greater satisfaction in life when we seek the good of others. You can't possibly create your own small world and control everything that happens there. You must learn to reach out to others in service and not concentrate on yourself alone.

Jesus Christ, our Lord, while He walked the earth derived satisfaction in serving others and not concentrating on Himself. This should be a lesson to us as His followers. This is our Christian calling and a way to find fulfillment in life. As Christ would act if He was physically here with us, we have to do the same and in doing so, we bring honor and glory to His name, and ultimately root out complacency in us.

In serving God, we have to do it with all our heart just as Jesus would do. When we allow the pain of others to be our pains, God attends to our own pains but when we keep living for ourselves alone, problems. As we focus on Christ through our love for others, God rewards us with joy, and a peace of mind. We were designed to serve others.

As Jesus did serve people during His sojourn on earth, we must do the same. By showing love to people around us, we point them to Jesus. That's our calling.

Exercise

How can you serve people in your neighborhood?

_____

_____

_____

_____

_____

How can you serve your community?

_____

_____

_____

_____

_____

_____

_____

What day is suitable for you to go out there and serve or show the love of Christ to people?

_____

_____

_____

Look around you; what do you have to serve? Who needs your love? What can you give away?

_____

_____

_____

_____

_____

How much can you take from your monthly income to serve others?

_____

_____

_____

Is there anything that appears to be limiting you from your service to God through people?

Yes [ ]   No [ ]

How do you intend to fix them so you can start serving others?

_____

_____

_____

_____

_____

_____

_____

_____

_____

Part 3: Thinking As Jesus Thinks

15 Who Do You Think You Are?

Our real journey in life begins when we accept Jesus as our Lord and personal savior. However, accepting Jesus doesn't make us impregnable to the troubles of this world, but our acceptance of Him and becoming part of the Light in Him can make us to come out of every challenge we find ourselves in the world. The more we give it up to Jesus, the more we find peace of mind and the more we shine in this dark world. Worry, fear and negative thoughts reign supreme in our life when we move away from Jesus to find satisfaction in the world.

We were made in God's image and the lies that the devil is making us to believe does not have power over us. When we accept Jesus, renounce the ways of the world and focus on Him alone, we enter our rest and lose from the grip of the devil. Even when we are still confronted with lies from the devil, we must learn to rebuke them and declare who we are in Christ. Brooding over the lies from Satan can have serious negative impacts on us. While we rebuke the devil and his lies, we must confess who we are in Christ. Satan has no power over our minds.

The Word of God is there for our training to face anything that life throws at us. We've been taught by the Word how to trust God even when we are going through difficult times. Instead of allowing negative thoughts drive us crazy, we can always look into the Word to see who we are or what we can do. Joy, peace, and victory over life circumstances can only be found in Jesus. At this point, you must get to study God's Word and know it for yourself.

Exercise

What lies is the devil trying to make you believe and what does the Word of God say about these lies?

_____

_____

_____

_____

_____

_____

_____

_____

_____

Identify Bible truths about your life in the following areas. Use a sticky note to write and paste them in your closet/room. Meditate on these scriptures every day.

Area of life	Scriptures for meditation
Health	
Protection	
Salvation	
Daily provision	
Breakthrough	
Finance	

16 Dangerous Thinking

The challenges of life have touched all of us. We've all been there; faced with the worst of life. However, God has always been there for us and He is good at all times. He alone can heal our broken heart or bring joy and beauty out of our brokenness.

One thing is clear, the challenges we go through today are not only unique to us, the Bible contains record of people who have gone through similar situations or even worse. One of such persons is Peter. Peter made a lot of mistakes. Even when Jesus had told him that he will deny Him three times, he couldn't do otherwise. Before the death of Jesus, he had denied Him thrice.

Irrespective, Peter still looked up to Jesus for strength and finish his race in Him. If Peter could do it, we can also do it regardless of our past errors. Turning to Jesus, forgiving, and forgetting our bad past experiences can make Jesus to strengthen and use us incredibly and making our brokenness become a history.

There are wonderful promises of God for us and we must learn to hold on to those promises and meditate on them to see that they come to pass in our lives. When we focus on Christ alone and not on our situations, we develop positive thoughts that ultimately affect our perception about life.

Ultimately, to maintain a positive focus on life, we need positive people around us and not people who would come to influence us negatively. Remember, iron sharpens iron. People who believe worrying and mongering fear is normal without focusing on Christ would always want you to think like them. Hence, choose positive friends who would in turn influence you positively and strengthen your focus on God. At all times, the result of putting your gaze on Jesus is freedom.

Exercise

List five challenges you are currently facing now?

_____

_____

_____

_____

_____

_____

_____

_____

_____

_____

_____

What scripture contains the promises of God you need to hold firmly about these challenges?

_____

_____

_____

_____

_____

_____

_____

_____

Mention friends that encourage you to focus on God and strengthens your faith in Him?

_____

_____

_____

_____

_____

_____

_____

Mention friends that usually concentrate on their situation only instead of focusing on Jesus to help solve their challenges?

_____

_____

_____

_____

_____

Who can you help to think positively about their life?

_____

_____

_____

_____

_____

Write a positive affirmation about who you are in Jesus.

_____

_____

_____

_____

_____

_____

_____

_____

_____

_____

_____

_____

_____

Tip: Meditate on these things before you to bed and when you wake up. Keep them in your heart.

Recommended Books

Prayer Journal: A 3-months guide to Prayer, Praise, and Gratitude featuring encouraging and faith-filled Bible verses

Link: mybook.to/MyPrayerJournal

Gratitude Journal: A Journal filled with Favorite Bible Verses

Link: mybook.to/GratitudeJournal

Made in the USA
Coppell, TX
08 July 2021